Heavy Words

by
Priscilla Akposi

Heavy Words

by Priscilla Akposi

Southern Arizona Press
Sierra Vista, Arizona

Heavy Words

By Priscilla Akposi

First Edition

Author: Priscilla Akposi
Editor: Paul Gilliland
Formatting: Southern Arizona Press
Cover Graphic: Matvey Doomchev from Pixabay

Published by Southern Arizona Press
Sierra Vista, Arizona 85635
www.SouthernArizonaPress.com

ISBN: 978-1-960038-48-7

Poetry

Dedication

Dedicated to God, my family, and parents who always believed in me.

Foreword

It's a glorious day when you get the honor of doing a foreword for a young poets first book. I have been an avid reader of Pri Lexa's poetry for some time. I find her poetry to be spiritual and incredibly profound. In talking with this young poet, she articulated her views on balance and order. That things can be both complex and simple and many times through our discussions we find our semblance of truth. There is order and chaos in our world, there are expectations, consequences, and opportunities all around us. The Author discusses cause and effect and parallels these thoughts in poetry that is both resonate and beautiful. Despite the Author's young age, she is quite mature in her thoughts and feelings surrounding her expressions in poetry. As if good and bad are mere opposites in the world, absent of intent, of consequences left to a society to make sense of these concepts with the help of God, of religion, our own experience and through the beauty of this world we live in. This book will inspire, and I believe force the reader to reevaluate how a world and the individual are drawn to balance. Thoughts that someone so young can articulate and expound on is inspiring and not an easy thing to do. As a published author of twelve books, I am excited to add this book to my collection and gain more insight and inspiration from this amazing poetry force. I invite the reader into the exploration of all of this and so much more. Seen through the keen eyes of a very talented poet that has created a very special book, "A rusted heart "

I am confident that this poet's beautiful words will touch you and lift up your spirit.

Robert R. Bradley, Jr., LCSW, LSATP
Family Therapist and Published Author

Introduction

Throughout my journey as a writer, I have come to understand the strength of balance in the human cycle. The cause - effect relationship that exists in our everyday encounter, the undeserving rewards we receive that sometimes burns our pride or fans to flame out determination. And with all these, even with all the pretense to be on the safe side with God and humanity, man falls into the coldness of the world rather than the warmth. Goodness no longer pierces the heart, one evil is enough to make man hate the world and himself. So, what if water is perpetually poured on water? It becomes rusted, the same thing when the heart succumbs to the cold of this world and forgets to keep a balance with the warmth. *Heavy Words* is penned with words that unveil the unseen warmth of the world, creating a balance to the weight of everything vile that resides in every broken heart and unites you with the peace within. I believe *Heavy Words* will be your guide to embrace that peace.

Priscilla Akposi (Pri Lexa)

Stunning versatility, alluringly beautiful, and eloquently executed — this is the essence in which Pri stains the soul's pages with. I have had the pleasure of watching her doodles turn into a skilled craft, then hang in the soul like a living Louvre for inked art. Her ability to captivate and awaken our inner emotive is unparalleled. For such a young woman to be able to articulate the hunger of poetry without starving the mind's palate is breathtaking. I would like to invite you all, confidently, to become a landmark for her pages to build history — your heart will never lose the legacy of her grace.
— Avant Avant-garde, Author, *Forged In Ink*

Pri Lexa is one of those rare gems that pop up when you aren't looking. An unassuming, gentle and sensitive soul, her wisdom and passion belies her youth. To her, poetry is an extension of the mind. An intrinsic part of what one could call a 'soul', of which this young lady has plenty of.
— Gavin Prinsloo, Author and Poet

Pri Lexa — A young poet that handles her Pen brilliantly and knows her way around a poem. The reader is sure to be absorbed in a journey that is spiritual and enlightening. Despite her young age, she is an old soul, full of inspiration and hope. This book is just a beginning for this amazing poet, mark my word, Pri Lexa is a literary force and her book, *Heavy Words* will be sitting prominently in my bookcase. Her words resonating in the readers heart. Much success to you Pri, you are an amazing talent.
— Robert R. Bradley, Jr., LCSW, LSATP, Family Therapist and Published Author

Pri Lexi is a phenomenal up and coming young author, who writes from the very depths of her being. Despite her youth, Priscilla's wisdom shines brightly from within in ink, making her remarkable calibre of beauty rare in this world amidst the youth today. It is an honour to have met Pri in the poetry world, and I wish her well with all her future endeavors, and that she will make her mark as a philosophical poetess, for she has much to offer the world.
— ©®Noora Salaam @ Writing EDEN (aka poetess RAW Diamond), Owner and Publisher

Budding poetess and upcoming author Priscilla with her phenomenal class and caliber has left indelible impression on poetic minds. Brilliance in literary artistry is bound to take her places, depth in her writings penetrate deep in the minds of readers, it's huge honour to be part of this beautiful literary venture. More success and accolades beautiful poetess @Pri Lexa proud of you work and your upbeat spirit. Best wishes for future endeavours.
— Gurjeet Kour Ghuman ©®

Bravely pouring out her emotions on the canvas of paper, Priscilla paints humanity's disdains and jarring reality. She writes to create a balance between that pain in your heart and your love for the beauty of the world. In her book titled *Heavy Words*, Priscilla's poems are really heavy because they bear the truth and reality of our lives that is sometimes overlooked. Best of all, she presents to the reader, peace on a golden platter, written in special poetry styles and with captivating poetic devices.
— Elizabeth O. Ogunmodede, Nigerian author, publisher, poet, website developer, graphic designer, and product designer.

Contents

Penalty	16
Tranquil	17
Mellow	18
Kaput	19
Sophisticated	20
Robust	21
Harmonious	22
Legendary	23
Construct	24
Banish	25
Frustration	26
Seize	27
Analysis	28
Provoke	29
Obligation	30
Disease	31
Coffee	32
Forbid	33
Language	34
Vision	35
Overwhelmed	36
Society	37
Historical	38
Ambition	39
Eruption	40
Pawn	41

Sailor 42
Veil 43
Memory 44
Faith 45
Persuasion 46
Acceptance 47
Tears 48
Equal 49
Hope's Death 50
Purpose 51
Ability 52
Say It! 53
In You 54
Why Within 55
It Happens 56
Love Cover 58
Seed 59
Normal 60
Pride's Death 61
Mea Culpa 62
Flying 63
Young Forever 64
Lesson 65
Infect 66
Good and Evil 67

Knowledge 68
Logic 69
Anger 70
Mistakes 71
Recount 72
Depth 74
Feelings 75
Word Battle 76
Simple Words 78
Karma 79
Not Normal 80
The Most Evil 82
Saving the Light 83
The One 84
Feel Me? 86
Burning Waters 88
Past on Fire 89
Born Anew 90
I'm an Open Book:
But Only I Can Read It 91
Music Danced 92
Accepting Beauty 93
It Is Not I 94
Faded Memories 96
— Just Say One Word — 97
A Flower 98

Unity 99
The Evil Eyes of the Heart 100
Music 101
The Plant Self 102
The Daisy Grew on the Dead 104
— Change — 106
All in the Eyes of a Baby 107
Sight 108
Conscious 109
Magic 110
Silence 112
Stepping Over 113
Imperfect 114
Giving Up 115
Write Path 116
Trash 118
Love Goes Away 119
Truth Rain 120
Fear ... 121
Heart Questions 122
The Risk 123
Teary Heart 124

About the Author 126

PENALTY

What caused our penalty?
A return of doom!
An arrest of our conscience warning!
The future of a wrong decision.
A goal of greedy pleasure.
The awaiting favor of justice.
The heat of our desperation.
We were warned!
Now we are rewarded!
A prize of no benefit.

TRANQUIL

With the wind that only whispered war ...
I blinked past the tears of turmoil ...

My feelings feigned a defense ...
Untouched by the words of pain and by the arrows of worries ...

In my heart you could hear the drop of water on a thousand oceans ...
I stood in the midst of a quarrel and yet I heard nothing ...

Camouflaged with stoicism ...
I remain placid ... tranquil.

A happiest moment in a story of horror.
I slept with my eyes closed under the sunset.

MELLOW

A rebound of anxiety.
A salvation to monotony.
Most cried.
But must be deprived of.
An arrest of anxious narcissism.
A requiem to coarse altruism.
A magnet to placid confession.
Here it comes, unease retribution.
Freedom from harshness.
Married to ease ... mellow dreams.

KAPUT

What's done is done.
No resurrection because it's gone.
Far from sight.
Impact of fright.
Can I replace it?
Bought again, maybe with a new face?
Sorry, they say.
You can't have it your way.
Because it is over.
Kaput, gone forever.

SOPHISTICATED

Staring at the mirror, she is everything you call stylish.
But deep within her eyes she knows she looks devilish.

Be elegant, dress sexy, do it right.
But all those are her biggest fears.

A girl should give it all to fit.
But all she wants to do is burn her closet.

Got all the tabs of richness.
But to her it's a wall of fakeness.

For she might look Sophisticated.
But deep within her heart it was all she hated.

ROBUST

She held a robust smile but couldn't fly herself to the moon.
She taunts the weakest blooms yet has to die too soon.
She was holding on so tight that it bruised her heart.
A sweet smile just couldn't come like that.
Reasons just couldn't tell her why!
Her hatred for the world's narcissism she had to deny.
A robust smile was not enough.
For truth to be heard you had to get tough.

HARMONIOUS

Good and evil battle for a win.
But deep in that fight is something vain.

Allow it be, allow it be.
Together their end let them see.

For if a man gets stung by a bee.
He will know the joy of being kissed by the sea.

Regret can be his sin.
If he doesn't get a balance sane.

Good and evil brushed his mind.
His life was rewarded with a harmonious kind.

LEGENDARY

Ye seek a polished lie.
Confined themselves to obnoxious fame.

Ye became the sorrow of another.
Because ye thought you were doing the world a favor.

Desperately seeking attention.
Ye took the path you once fret.

Ye hated thyself for not having what they had.
The courage to be you was all you seeked.

Now you are but a legendary fool.
The one everyone fears to come after.

CONSTRUCT

Pieces of my mind are scattered before me.
And I look for beliefs that would build my being.

The words I hear make up my decisions.
The things I see create possibilities and impossibilities.

The canvas of my mind is a mess.
I have to go pick and drop what is needed.

For my mind to become whole.
I construct it with all visibility, that makes me I.

I became a builder.
I stoop to conquer.

BANISH

A necessary evil lurks in our hearts.
And we are weakened by the voices in our head.

Gone with the wind we seek refuge.
But in this world, we cannot find it.

Everything around us invites chaos.
So very little is our strength.

We are forgetting the meaning of birth.
Summarizing our dreams in death.

Because the world chose to banish good.
And knocked on the gate of evil.

FRUSTRATION

The moon and the sun dance around each other.
But when the sun goes to sleep all the moon feels is frustration.

So, it loses its shine at night.
It moans in pain out of sight.

The earth will cry from darkness.
For she has met with her limitation; darkness.

The night gets cold.
Men lose their sanity in the moon's blinding sadness.

Because the moon for a day, couldn't meet with her lover.
The sun.

SEIZE

Turn me in and out.
But please don't seize my smile.

It is the freest gift I have received.
And the cheapest present I can afford.

It is the only friend I have.
The only thing I can't live without.

It is the biggest pride I have.
And the holiest ground I walk.

It is the sharpest sword alive.
It is the only thing that pierces the soul; a smiling goodness.

ANALYSIS

She knows not her purpose.
For she was born out of an analysis.

It was written about her before birth.
And concluded of her after death.

A life nailed to prejudice.
Had cost her a river of tears.

Oh me! oh my! She cried.
"Why can't I just die".

From under the spotlight.
She longs to live her own life.

PROVOKE

I love them.
But do not provoke my heart to regret it.

Reciprocate the fragrance of my smile.
And know that it is for you and only you.

Be proud of my touch.
For I hold yours as the greatest trophy ever won.

Forgive my imperfections.
For I adore yours like they were the purest gold.

All this does.
And we'll live together, a stimulant to each other's
temperance.

OBLIGATION

Is it an obligation for my heart to love again?
Cause I tell you that time it broke I still can't find the pieces!

Is it a must to take your hands?
Cause I tell you that time you shrugged it off, I can't lift it!

Must! Must! Must!
It is a must that I know who I trust!

Force! Force! Force!
Don't make me do it if I don't want to!

For I tell you my heart is tired!
It refuses to work for you!

DISEASE

I know a certain neighbor!
They live so far but yet so near!

They died from a selfless disease!
They cry themselves to sleep!

Yet they wake and help the sick!
Yet they were strengths to the weak!

Oh how funny that there is a poorest from the poor!
How sad that they all look at each other with scorn!

These neighbors chose to be the cures!
In a world where evil was pure!

COFFEE

Shall I lose or gain sleep from your love?
Don't mistake this as my choice!
I am only under the influence!
I had all the choices!
But I chose to lose sleep from thinking of you!
Your smile is like coffee!
It leaves me drunk.
To a potion that is not alcohol!
I bask in your cup!

FORBID

The journey of life gets too tough.
Sometimes it forbids her to know that she's not enough.

She fears being optimistic.
Because she gets scared of the outcome.

Why she jumped was obvious.
But the pretense will not permit her condolences.

Everything was taken from her!
Abused and forgotten for a long time.

All of this was not her will.
For she struggled, but was not allowed to be okay!

LANGUAGE

Ye do not understand what my heart says.
For the language my heart speaks is gibberish to your mindset.

Complicated as the wave, is the way you like it.
Harsh as the sun is the way you want it!

Pay attention to my simple words!
For all tongues to understand " I love you."

Teach yourself to understand all the signs.
For when I call I want an answer!

A communication whispering one thought.
All love is the same!!

VISION

The songs of our hearts have been plagiarized.
The visions of our parents' failed dreams.

The memories of our beautiful future we dream ...
Has been robbed from us.

Here we are, now children of the night.
With a future so opaque that it's blind.

Growing up as adults.
That we do not know the joy of a child.

Forever we dream.
But it's hard to find a reality.

OVERWHELMED

You stayed so near to our hearts.
We break at the thought of you no longer here.

The memories of your smile will forever taunt us!
This is what we fear.

Your demise is a breath taken from us!
We are void of thoughts and reasons.

Goodbye would never be uttered.
Our lips would sin from it.

We are overwhelmed by your presence.
That we tremble at the thought of your absence.

SOCIETY

Only eighteen but still too naive.
Still controlled by society.

Yet still far from dreams that are seen.
But still so close in belief.

"Act your age," they say!
But how so, when I've never been this age before.

Achieved courage but they argued my wealth.
Housed in confusion but so sure of what I want.

Their death is near!
Because now I close my ears to their words.

HISTORICAL

Thou repeated the same mistake.
To become what you could not make.

You desire thyself an artifact to be stared upon.
But cry in pain when ye takest that turn.

They regret stare back at ye from the mirror.
Thy pain continues as tomorrow, never ending.

The point of thy sacrifice was wasted.
Thy outcome ye loathed.

Because ye forgot that your beauty was not supposed to be historical.
For being thy truest self is the greatest memorial.

AMBITION

Look and you will find our determination.
We strive for things beyond our power.

We indulge in mischievous conversations.
When we cry for all that would hold us together.

We become puppets to frustration.
What placates the society is dangerous.

For what we cannot achieve we lay to condemnation.
The risk was all for admirers.

Good was our ambition.
But we collapsed to a polished greed and all became liars.

ERUPTION

Verses were born the day they witness a flower bloom.
Imagination was born the day they watched that beautiful view.
A single verse of laughter!
Created an eruption of happiness and wonder.
Not much was to be done.
It was the day they all ceased to mourn.

PAWN

A game where the victim does all the work.
A pushover of time and space we all become.

Hungered for a lie of our own belly.
A tradition that was never arranged.

With wisdom that has no purpose.
If there is a purpose, it is only for the tears of our eyes.

With no mercy they fight.
With a laughter that only mocks us.

We remain a pawn in their sick game.
Except we see the hidden agenda in their plot.

SAILOR

As imagination is my biggest nation.
I'm a sailor of your heart.
Without my acceptance you drown into rejection.
A sad fate caused by a shadowed bearing.
Listen to my instructions if you want our ship to sail.
Darling, that ship is my only home.
I won't let it sink.

VEIL

Call a spade a spade oh little trickster.
Set the right alarm as thy reminder.

Thou built a room with no walls.
A house with no fence.

But placed a watchman at an invisible tower.
Surrendered to thy greed handler.

Because thou was covered by a veil of your past.
Thou chose to live a simple lie; ‘it’s okay’.

MEMORY

Remember!
I wish not that you forget.

Remember!
To take my poems as your handset.

Remember!
It is possible to be a winner in a contest with ten thousand people.

Remember!
There is no foolishness in poetry.

Remember!
My words are a memory I try to have you recall with your own story.

FAITH

What is your faith?
When you can't demonstrate it.

Words go a mile,
But an action of ten thousand.

The fallen remains abase,
But his faith is proven when he desires a lifting.

If it is wanted, say it.
If it is needed, do it.

For your faith is pointless if you do nothing.

PERSUASION

Every destiny in God comes with a persuasion
What say you?

The initial plan
Cannot be aborted.

No matter the negligence.

If it not the initial,
It can't be the end.

For an end is only possible through a beginning.

ACCEPTANCE

Peace within is true acceptance.
What peace have you if others accept you, but you detest you.

Peace within is true acceptance.
What gain do you have when you smile outside, but cry inside.

An historical fool you'll become,
If you yearn for a place in the world, then a place in your heart for yourself.

TEARS

Why wait for others to pick your tears?
Many times we cry ourselves to sleep ...
Oftentimes we do many good things to be disgusted by ourselves.

We ...
Trust all
Trust none ...
Befriend all ...
Yet I have no friends ...

We enjoy it but not to foolishness ...
Hear oh ye wise ...
That only the strong cry ...
For they have the desire to save.
The strength to pick their tears.

EQUAL

The right is considered a wrong
The wrong a right.

The strong dares you to tempt justice,
The weak dares you to live.

Controversy drags your heart to indecisiveness.
Your excuses become your comfort.

Know now ...
That with ignorance is suffering.
And with knowledge is equality.

HOPE'S DEATH

At the presence of life,
There seems to be hope.

Seems?
Yes ...
For some still don't believe there is surely hope.

So, it does.
Trying to make you see the unseen.
Trying to make you believe the unbelievable
Trying to make you understand your potential

It was killed by fear
A distorter of your vision.
God called,
You answered not.
It died the day you stopped believing
It is hope ...
It died in your heart.

PURPOSE

Man comes to a point of self-hatred,
When he can't give himself what he wants.

The inability of seeing his potential,
Creates a doubt on his existence.
He feels worthless.

Unless he understands the true meaning of purpose,
He will continue living in competition.

But ...
If he finds what he can do,
He won't waste his time on what he 99 cannot do
And if he stops in what be has done,
He won't discover what he can do further.

ABILITY

Our abilities can never be exhausted.
To be the best you must conquer your quest.
Doing well in your task is all that matters.

SAY IT!

You never know
If what your heart says is true
Until you say it
With your mouth.

IN YOU

I won't be afraid if I lose you.
Why?
Because I never had a friend in you ...

WHY WITHIN

Why act so shy?
Why do your tears drop in a cry?
Why do your dreams hide beneath your eyes?
Your touch is oh so vile
Insecure may I pry
Redeemed must I die
I seek the peace of mind

As time passes by
With eyes blue as the sky
I succumb to the bittersweets of lies
Being led to a fake paradise
I can't die on the devil's time
The intimacy with the truth I seek to find

The song of my heart I seek to rhyme
But the lyrics to them I fear the line
A million reasons for my why's
Even darkness seemed to shine
The flowers sprung high above light
To seek truth in heavens paradise
To the why's within your eyes ...

IT HAPPENS

It happens
The feeling happens
Nothing necessarily causes it
It just happens

The feeling of uselessness
The worthless feeling
The undeserving feeling
The not good enough feeling
The feeling of being in control
The sad feeling
The depression happens
The tears happen
The weakness happens
And when it happens
It hits hard ... Very hard ... Deadly hard

Sometimes we do not see the people around us
We forget about the footprints
We are surrounded but alone
It happens
All the time
And when it happens, we have no other choice but to feel it
It's okay to feel them
Cry it out
Hit the pillow
Scream it out
It's ok not to be okay
But

I tell you, my friend,
Yes you
Sometimes we need to feel the unfeeling
We need to see the unseen
We need to take a step
We need to create our strength
If no one is your strength.
Be your strength
And if you think you don't have a strength
Look at your weaknesses
And in that weakness, you will find your strength.
Keep pushing
Tired?
Then it's okay
Take a rest
But keep pushing
Even if I'm not there with you
My prayers will be with you
Just keep pushing
Be the change you need
Know that troubles will come
Life sucks but not all the time
Because
It happens.

LOVE COVER

To trust is hard but not impossible
To love is easy but hard to find
Our love will be an umbrella
In the rain of distrust
I'll risk a smile
To be a fool of love.

SEED

You are but a seed.
That dies and springs forth to become a tree.
The hurt won't kill.
If it tries to
Die to it and you'll grow better.

NORMAL

Stupidity is when you think
You can be normal
In this abnormal world

PRIDE'S DEATH

A mighty wind twirled at the feet of pleasure.
And like a drunk bride our pride fell.
Married to humility,
The two are perfect.
Mistake it not for inferiority.
The two, imperfect.
If all minds thought alike,
We would not declare war against each other's hearts.
If all songs were melodies,
Then dance would not exist.
If the moon dances with the sun,
The earth would sing alone.
A pierce to your heart,
You died at night,
But you yearned for the light of the day.
If only you were patient,
Then I would have been by your side.
I trade my inferiority for humility.
For I was tired of not being able to 'say', everything
silence stole from me.
I drink the wine of pain.
And like a phoenix my courage rose,
A perfect requiem for pride.

MEA CULPA

My fault ...
I remember my trust.
A trick of time was a must
I sent my prayers to a judge.

The only mistake I made was lie
To discover a truth
To build an empire of trust.

A trust built-in lie
Surely would burst
There is no certainty of its stay
A seed planted in hate can never survive in the weather of love

Forgive me
For it is my fault we ended up this way ...
Regretting.

FLYING

Oh, my little butterfly.
Teach me how to fly
For if I stay on this ground
I would surely die ...

YOUNG FOREVER

"Act your age," they say.
But they don't know that this is me ...
I'm never leaving my little league ...
I'll never grow old
I'll keep growing younger ...
With a beautiful soul, body, and spirit.

LESSON

The lessons that are learnt from change.
Will lead a man to self-care.

And if he creates a connection with the family of his mind
And have the power of gratitude.

There will be a breakthrough.
For a creation of motivation.

INFECT

The chaos in the world,
Cause an intentional infection in the heart of many.

Cold as ice we freeze.

But if allowed ...
The warmth of good melts it away

GOOD AND EVIL

The two must exist.
The two have been alive.
And it takes one to kill the other.

Evil builds the walls in our soul
Good pierces the soul.

From a cry we experience the joy of a smile.
And from loss we appreciate gain.

They are inevitable.
There is one.

Only when you understand this.
Can you appreciate life?

KNOWLEDGE

Preserving … a knowing that brings elation.

Destroying … a knowing that brings sadness.

Ignorance is a bitter knowledge

For thou know something but it is NOTHING.

Thou search and do not find.
You have all yet lacked.

Your significance is insignificant.
Because you know but know the wrong thing.

Truth I tell you is not bitter but edifying.

Knowing the wrong thing is true ignorance.

LOGIC

Not epically right.
Something believed in sight.

Born out of curiosity.
Planted in the conclusion of man necessity.

What comforts the philosophers?
But their fallacies are believed.

Through a medium called YOU.
An ignorant you.

Logic lies when it says it is the truth.
When in reality it is a fallacy not willing to lose to the truth.

ANGER

A necessary answer to pain
An open reaction to wrongs ...

It hails you not in your plight
Entices you to take revenge

It focuses your mind on the errs
Erases the resilience of your tears

Hails you to sin
Conforms you to become your offender

Tell you a distorted story ...
That which no one understands

Do you understand?

MISTAKES

Torments our sanity ...
Convinces our insanity to be on their side ...

Perfections destroyer ...
Sorry increases its pride ...

A necessary darkness lurking ...
Unwanted lies revoked ...

Imperfections reminder ...
A curse to our sanity

A means to mold ...
If the truth should be told.

RECOUNT

Snarls of deceit
Growls of aggression
A heart of jealousy
Giving birth to hate

The scriptures has told of the aimless movement
Of he who walks to and from
Looking for who to steal, kill and destroy
What a pity that a heart is filled with such thoughts

Mind you, beware that the devil
Is not he who comes with a hideous face and horns
Hell is only but an empty space
Because all the devils now prauls and lives in the heart of men

Beware of men
For they will deliver you into the temple of their hate
Busy bodies in others matters
Pursuers of the fortunes of the good
Those who hate understanding
Those who let their ignorant rule them
Those who seek not knowledge

Corruption now rules the day and night
Because men are blinded to the true darkness of evil
Burning others on stake ... Claiming they are right and the others are wrong ...
Claiming they are righteous and the others are sinners
When all along they are the true evil in heart
Only plotting others' demise ...

The greatest evil is mostly underrated ... Taken as a good
But that which is good is taken as the wrong
But although the pangs of rain
The affliction and temptation ...
The troubles of the devil ...
The Lord is coming for his people
And everyone will be saved ...

DEPTH

From your sleep

From your sleep
Ye shall know the death
Its never too late to be early
Never forgotten to be remembered

Laying in deep
The greatest truth of rebirth
The fake friend greatest excuse is busy
There is always a lost to be discovered

From the greatest sleep a dream is born
Awakened ,the dream comes true
Determined the dream is established
Staying true the dream never dies

Never fear the silence of sleep tugs
The moment in life when it seems you exist not
For then you will find what is true
What and who exists around you ...

FEELINGS

It was a liability
But my only ability ...
To feel
The day I stop
I die ...

WORD BATTLE

What to do?
I'm curious
But yet I'm afraid
These questions keeps churning and burning inside my head
Keeps knocking to get out

What to do?
Do I run from them?
These words in my head
Are they really me ?
Are they true

I walk alone
I sit alone
But these conversations in my head arise ...
My imagination ...
My fears ...
Sometimes it's terrifying
Sometimes it's fascinating
Should I be afraid of them?

No
Maybe not
Maybe I could just have a little chat with it
Maybe I could find myself through this conversation
I will talk about it ...
I own my thoughts ...
I am to decide what we should talk about
If the words go too far?
I could shut it out
Shut the words out
I'll say ... shhhh be quite
By getting out there
Or listen to that music

Yes, I am those words
It is my subconsciousness
I will shut it out
When it needs to be shut
But I will never run away from them ...

SIMPLE WORDS

They travel a long journey
Touching the grounds of souls
Rebuking the fears of a foe
Supply riches of sweetness like honey

Please ... Sorry ... Thank you
Though appears mere and simple
Holds an impact of pure bliss and miracle
Not complex, saying the simple words sometimes is all that will do

I adore ... I praise ... I love
Simple and sweet sometimes does the magic
Tender and true ... it brings an ease to the mind of conflict
Felt in the bosom of the heart and soul in soothes

Think not of my simple words as ignorant
For once a time a word has to be said to unfold thousands
A name has to be called for recognizing
Behold those words as the souls rants and grants

My vocabulary is empty
With these few and simple words
I don't mean to get under your skin
But in your soul kingdom I want to walk in
Let my simple words soothe your obvious reality

Give ears to my simple tongue
Not saying much
But it feels and will do much
Read and listen to my simple words of songs ...

KARMA

Fret not that you are loved less
For it is because you have Loved more
A day will come
In which
Your power of love
Will overcome
Their love for power
You that has watered
Shall be watered ...

NOT NORMAL

I cried
You laughed

You pushed me to the ground
How could we walk together?

You left scars of your words on me
That cut deeper than razor

My screams were to deaf ears
Loud enough to dry my throat
But you ignored it like you ignore the pleas of my heart

You choose the path ...
... I followed
Why is the truth whatever you decide
Why is the calling whatever you name

I grew tired of following
I wanted to walk my own path
I found my purpose but you called it a joke
I found my peace but you called it not normal
I pursued my dreams and you called me weird

Now if only you would get your butts down
Look around you
See the different colors , shape and plains, hills and valleys

You would understand that not every feet will fit the same shoe
That we all have our path to walk
Either to lead or follow

And if one choose to lead ... let them lead ... for it is their path
And if one chooses to follow ... Lead them well .. with love, peace, and truth
Not in force , hate. and torture
That my dear is not normal ...

THE MOST EVIL

Is it okay to knock and not open
I'm afraid to wonder to a land of hate ridden

I'm afraid to seek and not find
It's not my fault my heart doesn't accept a dislike

This confusion is so confusing
The way others lie and judge is really not amusing

Don't play me, I'm not a game
I won't be a fool for those lies again

Is it fair that a puzzle becomes a maze
That a presence all along was a deceiving absence daze

I ask for help, a true helper
Turns out I was seen as a gold digger

Why is the most genuine seen as the most evil
The most battered seen as the cold hearted civil

When all along the most evil is not understanding
Not seeing what truly needs a recognizing

The truth is whatever you decide
But no, please read in between the lines

For the most evil is not what it seems instead
It's mostly underrated ...

SAVING THE LIGHT

There is no darkness
Without a light
And there is no light
Without a light

Thou art the fiery flame
Speaketh thou water?
....
Do you seek to keep the balance
Or
Do you disrupt the balance
It is a must that my ...
... power of love and balance
Overcome my ...
... Love for power and control
Verily ... There is no perfect angel ... There is no perfect demon
There is always evil but there is always good ...
... A balance must be ... Will be ... Can be ... if we know it
Then we will be prepared for the worst ... And enjoy the best ...

Thou are like the fiery flame ...
Speaketh thou water!!!!!!
For in this light we are controlling the darkness
And in this darkness we are
Saving the Light ...
... To bring balance ...

THE ONE

Yes, you will die
But I won't be the one
To kill you
You will fall
But I won't be the one
To push you
You will drown
But I won't be the water
That fills your lungs
You will cry
But I won't be the one
Who causes the tears to fall

How many times?
But a thousand times
They are those out there
Who wants to do this to you
But I swear I won't be the one
It will always come but
I don't want to be the one who causes it

I want and need to be the one
Who helps you live
The one who pulls you
When you fall
The breath that safes you
From drowning
The one who wipes your tears
And brings you a smile.

How many times?
But a thousand times
Your bubbles of hope
I wanna be
We will be screaming volumes
Of help and communication
For yes I tell you
They will be bad
They will be an evil
A thousand of evil
But they will always be
The one good
The one peace
I wanna be
THE ONE ...

FEEL ME?

Fragments ...
Piece after piece
Broken
The one who breaks
Or the one who mends
Who are you?

Do you feel what I feel
Or do you stir what I feel
Testing ...
Everyday seeking and searching
To find
To know

You are human like me
Right?
Or is it me just imagining
That you feel what I feel
That you see the unshed tears I cry
Or my broken self I hide

Do you feel me?
Do you
Hear me?
Will we
Wither
Together
Smile
For a while
Or always
In all ways
Do you feel me?
Or what do I feel?
Cause I know if you did
Then you would do to me
What you would want to be done to you
You would make me feel
What you want to feel
For I tell you
No man wishes to feel pain
Even a masochist yearns for peace
So ...
Do you feel me? ...

BURNING WATERS

She said
"if I would love
I would love like burning waters
Because nothing will quench it
It doesn't matter if I'm not loved back
The fire of that hate
Can never quench the burning of my waters
I will kill them with kindness
Live with them in peace
And love them like burning waters ..."

PAST ON FIRE

My past is on fire
Burning away every single day
Every single moment
Every second ...

Tick ...
Tick ...
The clock is reminding me
Flames of fire
Colliding
To bring a full force
Of present and future

What is gone is gone
Yes?
Yes
Will I remember them
Yes?
Yes
Always never forgetting
But never bringing it back
Ashes on the ground
All my cool is gone
Replaced with this heat from my burning past

Yes, my past is burning
With the fire of my present
With the hope of my future
My past
Is on fire ...

BORN ANEW

Mend my spites
Right my wrongs
Shift
Break
Get together?
Yes
Okay

Healing from the hurts
Finding a purpose
Find
Know
Am I getting a purpose?
Yes
Okay

Being real
Growing
Finding
Knowing
Who I really am
Blooming
Germinating ...

Getting who I really am
To full reality
Being born anew
To a new dimension
Knowing my worth
Smiling over a loss
Cause I know I'm getting a new self
My new me
Has been
Born anew ...

I'M AN OPEN BOOK: BUT ONLY I CAN READ IT

page after page
Ink poured in sync
Forfeiting the sage
My mind holds the words

I'm an open book
But I bet
You don't read me
That's why you don't understand my look

Story of my life
Begins with me
Journey of my mind
Travels in me

Alone time
Serenity ...
Slowly ... I'm understanding
The plot of my own story

My words tell my story
Of yesterday
The words are locked in my head
Left for only me to tell

For really
I'm an open book
But only I can read it ...

MUSIC DANCED

My darling friend
She sang you a lullaby
Did you sleep?
Like a spider web
You wrapped around her feet
Entangled she was in your song

Her voice holds the key
To her song
Her feet holds the moves
To her dance

For I tell you
Music danced
When she danced
Music was fulfilled
When she understood ...
The lyrics behind the beat ...

ACCEPTING BEAUTY

Acceptance is beauty
Beauty is acceptance
Beauty is when you accept your flaws and scars and know that
Your flaw is your beauty
Your scar is your mark of resilient
Our flaws makes us unique
It makes us different
You've gotta know this
That everyone has a certain good
But not everyone has your flaws
No one is like you
In your flaws lays your beauty
Because a flaw is a mirror to seeing ones beauty
It is a door that opens to the kingdom of your gods and goddesses within
And this can only
Start from within
Look at your flaws and don't see a mistake
But see a beauty that only the eyes of the wise can behold and understand
See those scars in your body
And don't see what makes you ugly or battered
But see it as a remembrance of yesterday's pain and why you need to keep fighting for tomorrow joy
Fall in love with yourself
Think of yourself as what you truly are
Be yourself
Accept your flaws
For when you accept your flaws
Then you are accepting your beauty
It all starts from within ...

IT IS NOT I

*Trigger warning *

"Take that mirror"
They say
"Look at yourself, you pathetic creature"
They laugh
"You have freckles"
"You are too fat"
"You are too thin"
"You are big eyes"
"You have big cheeks"
"You look so lame"
They laugh again

Their eyes never wants
What lays within
Their words always a torment
We think
"No, I'm not good enough, what they is true"
We hate ourselves
They have achieved their goal
They have crushed our self esteem
They have their hands around our neck
Preparing to strangle us
To the death of self-hate
They have held us so tight
That our minds start thinking
What they say
Our eyes start seeing
What they want us to see
We take up a mirror
And instead of seeing our truest self
We see what they call us
A pathetic creature

But today
Let's do this
Let's take up that mirror and say
IT IS NOT I
Let's take up that mirror and look through
Our own eyes
Our own eyes would be there to picture the 'you' that needs to be seen
Not the one that has been
Painted with lies

Let's break that mirror of their lies
And repeat
IT IS NOT I
I am thee
Whom you are afraid of
The one who keeps you thinking awake at night on how to take me down
The one whom you look at everyday
To find flaws
And when you don't
You find my uniqueness and call it weird
I AM ME
IT IS I

FADED MEMORIES

Memories never leave us
People come and go
She has always watched them
Leave ...

Where are you now?
Inside her head?
Inside her chest?
Locked in her heart

Remembering ...
Is it bad to do so
Sometimes she wishes to relive those memories
But sometimes, there are some better left faded
Buried under the souls scar

The memories of pain
She will never forget, she keeps it as a reminder of the passer-by deceit
But those sweet little memories
Of happiness and joy
She holds tights
Never to let go
Those memories of pain and joy
She holds them dear as a reminder
Of tomorrows date with destiny
She designs those memories with marks of resilient

With the pains
She learns and grow
With the joy
She continues to flourish
memories may fade but they never leave us
They are reminders of growth ...

— JUST SAY ONE WORD —

Say one word
And let me hear thousands
Let me sought
And let me reach many hands
Let the stars drop
And let me pick them up
Let the wind blow
And let my skin glow
I write not for the likes
But for the heart
I speak with time
To consort with the mind
Let me get lost
And let there be no rust
Let me close my eyes
But let me still see the shines
Let my dress
Be not depress, but impress
Let my hair
Caress my neck snare
Let me levitate
With a meaningful temperate
— just say one word —

A FLOWER

Can I tell you how my flower do feels?
Soft the petals more as her soul do aches
To be given attention she can't conceal
All for her growth, self-company and love sake
Sometimes she shimmers with a bad wither
Often times her roots are broken for nothing
Forgotten, her beauty is not remembered
Bringing the dreadful mind fulfilling ding
But faded not her beauty to the eyes
Lifting everyday towards the heavens gate
Looking always for an attention love smile
With a soft mind blowing sweet
temperate
Still her grace grows unending with no plight
Still her beauty, enchanting to any sight ...

UNITY

Can't our hands be tied
Until they die
Can't they fight with a mighty cry
Why spit
When given a togetherness
Knowing that there sounds
That kept us bound
Memories
All with shredding rounds

I know you think my hands are dead
Rotting with no purpose
You don't see the roots growing back to life
You don't see the rising of butterflies
When I hold my pen
You don't see the circle of revival
But I see it
For they do not die to die
They died to live ...

THE EVIL EYES OF THE HEART

Do you believe the heart
Sees evil?
Yes or no
You wouldn't know until you experience and see it
evilness
As it love fiercely
So does it hate with so much force
It hits harder than a hammer
The embers of it hotter than fire
When it is stained with mud
It carries the most dirt
Be careful and mindful of the evil eye of the heart
For it looks with mischievousness and deceit
Cause not a trigger to it
Be careful.
.

MUSIC

Music invited me to her cabana
I got addicted to her melodies
Corrupting my boredom
Like a bad ass belladonna

Dear music
She held my hands
And pulled me into the dance floor
To dance with her
Her moves and beats
Are filled with mighty body flows and sounds

Music
She made me cry
Tears of understanding
Her mysterious lyrics
All with soft petals
Of her touch on my soul with a beautiful pry

Dear music
Let's runaway
To a galaxy
With our fantasy
As our guide
For an adventurous ride ...

THE PLANT SELF

If I be a plant
Then every day I would
Water myself till I grow to the fullest
For the scripture says
He that waters
Shall be watered

Dead I lay
My energy wasted and exhausted
I've been buried in so much hate
I lay there
In an ever-tiring sleep
I have watered
Till my water runneth out
So, I worry not
For I can't be watered except I die to sprout back again
For strength comes when I'm weak
Although my strength drained to a zero
I'll be raised to a hero

Everything happens for a reason
Falling to rise
Poor to be made rich
 Wounded to be healed
Crying to get a better smile
Nothing is for naught
This challenge was faced for a better testimony tomorrow
So, it is
And so
 If I be a plant
 I care not if I wither
  For I know the sun will shine back
And I'll be watered by my Lord
So dead I lay
 But alive I will arise together with HIM
  For the seed won't sprout until
  It dies ...

THE DAISY GREW ON THE DEAD

Passing over grounds
To this
In a very deserted
Ground of death
Is the reason
The daisy chose to grow on the dead

Battered to the dust
Depression and anxiety
Sucked and ate
All the flesh out
Leaving a very pathetic
Deadly corpse
Who have tried to
Survive
Who has and will
Always be
Resilient

Thus the reason
The daisy chose to
Abide with it
For it has perceived
And observed
It resonates
It knows
It strife of survival
The flesh that decayed from it bones
Has supplied and given
A great deal of nutrients
To the ground

So, it's resilience was not for naught
It has died every winter
But survived all the weather
For it's ground was rich with nutrients of resilience
And so the daisy grew on the dead
Because out of the dead
Comes out
An
Alive ...

– CHANGE –

Change mocks us everyday
With her ever revolving grace
That's right
She comes every moment
Knocking on our door
With a graceful enticement to the soul
Her pain a magnificent beauty
Her joy a glorious reality
She is that storm
That don't seem to go away
She is constant
Appealing to the soul that understands
That she will always come

Thump ... Thump ... Thump
That's the sound of her heels
Marching everyday
Wondering in every man's house
But if you can only be calm
If you can calm the rage of the storm of your soul
For if your storm clashes with hers
There will be nothing left
But an ocean
Filled with death
Let her storm pass by
For surely it will pass by
And then you will see
Her waters calmed
The beauty of her sea
Peace will be felt
And you will be glad you watched her
And know that there is no storm that can't be calmed
And that there is always a
– CHANGE –

ALL IN THE EYES OF A BABY

The eyes of a baby
Have you ever wondered
What lays within
In their bosom of bashfulness
Languages are symphonies
In the demon they see no evil
But the hidden smile
For they smile back
They look with pure adoration
Soothing even the dirtiest mind
In their eyes there is no hate
But pure love
A rich peace
They see your little smile
And turn it to a big laughter
Their pretty little fingers
Holding just a finger of you
With nothing
But
Pure admiration
Of how big there are
This story lay
All in the eyes of a baby.

SIGHT

She said to me
Perfection is not the absence of imperfections
It is the presence of both
To create a balance
For a true self ...

CONSCIOUS

I thought the day was bright
Until I saw the galaxies of the night
It was always there to lead me to my brightest tomorrow.

MAGIC

Suddenly it happens
Suddenly it vanishes

What can you see, a fallen picture, a risen memory, a misguided mind, or a loved branch

What do you feel, a sparky soothing, one with fire, one that takes you higher, makes you sober or gives you peace

It was everything you needed
What you wanted
But eventually
It becomes everything you detest
What you never wanted

Oh yes it happens like Magic
A serene feeling
 Beautiful
  Endearing
A reminder of your desire
But like magic too
Sometimes
It gets dark
 With lies
  Hideous images
Manipulative
A reminder of your foolish consumer

May the magic flow
But only from within
The core dripping
Pure images
Burning like embers
Giving you a December feeling
Just like that
The magic will happen
Which will leave you
Awed in wonder ...

SILENCE

Don't speak
  Silence says
Reminding the moment
Talks of no understanding
Hears of no listens
Writing but no one to read
Songs but no voice to sing
Shhh ...
Sound
  Is in animosity
  With silence
For with it there is no silence
The only sound that should be heard is the sound of your mind
And you speaking to you
Then
Talks would be understood
There would be a listening
You will read the words of your mind
And your voice will sing that song
But shhh ... silence says
  Speak to yourself

STEPPING OVER

Right now
One of us is crying
One of us is smiling
One of us is weak
One of us is sick
One of us has a grin on their face.
One of us is in a comfortable place
One of us is not in a comfortable place

We all are facing many situations right now
Right now
One of us is broken hearted
One of us is getting sober
One of us should be stepping over

I know you are feeling low
I know you are so tired
Tired of everything
I know you want to be happy
Even if you are lonely
Believe me I know

If you want the light
You must run to it
If you want to leave the hole
You must crawl out of it
It you want to smile you must twitch your lips
If you want to let the feeling out
Shout it out
Scream it out
Cry it out
Laugh it out
Write it out

You must take a step in stepping over

IMPERFECT

She has hurt, she has been hurt
She has made someone cry and she has cried
She has made others smile and she has smiled
She has made others feel stupid and she has felt stupid
She has made others feel talented and she has felt
talented
Recognized imperfections ...

She is not fine
She is not okay
She looks around and find she is surrounded but alone
She smiles a lot but she cries the most
She acts crazy a lot but she is the one who sits there alone
Watching the stars and the moon go by
Sun rises
Sun sets
She is being looked at weirdly if she dances with no music
But the music
Is the moment elation
She is not perfect
She strife to be good
To follow the heart of Lord God
When she offends
She forgives
To be forgiven
Forgive her imperfections ...

GIVING UP

Sometimes she feels like giving up
But what is she giving up on ?
This confusion
Being confused
Is really confusing
She doesn't know anymore
The purpose
Is diminishing
This hopelessness
Is making her go crazy
She wants to cause a wreck
No one to converse with
Her mind is her only medium to start a conversation
Giving up
Where does she start?
When there is nothing to give up on ...

WRITE PATH

Are you on a write path
Oh yes, I can see
Don't tell me
To take
An explore shun
For in it
Will I find
My fasts in nations
Now what is in my mind is mine
Now I leave you to start
Mining your mind
For the hidden treasure of your words ...

This silence is so loud
And I don't know what to do
This silence has no mouth
Yet it speaks though

When it speaks
It speaks tranquility
If you listen carefully
You will find your inner self
That has longed to be found

Be not afraid of it
Listen ,for it will speak the truth
Be cautious of the mind deceit
For it might try to hide the truth
But listen

And speak to it
For when you speak to it
You listen to yourself
For it speaks tranquility
        It speaks self care
        It speaks acceptance
For it is a Speaking Silence

TRASH

I am that poem
You threw away
Because you don't appreciate poetry
I chose my path
Rebuking every bond
That was not meant to be tied

I behold my path
I am that piece of art
I am that poem
So read those lines ...

LOVE GOES AWAY

What do you feel
Is it pity or love
Do you pour it all away
Like it was only a dirty water
Is it true that
Love goes away ...

The reminder is always there
The consumer is always here
Where will you be
When they are drowning
For with you does
Love goes away ...

Do your bones beg
Your lungs beg
When you see the hungry
The helpless
Do you confirm to them
That love goes away ...

Are you the defender or accuser
Abuser or saviour
Are you the battered and bruised
Yes maybe you are
I am, either

Let not this love go away
If it should
May it leave to abide in another
That truly
This love does not really
GOES AWAY ...

TRUTH RAIN

I need the rain of truth
  To fall in the place of peace
Now truth rain on me
  For if more lies keep pouring
  Then I'll drown in the sea of Hate ...

FEAR ...

Fear is inevitable
But avoidable
A natural phenomenon
Even
The bravest needs safety
The rich has it
And then you come to make me fear
Go face your own fears and leave me to mine ...

HEART QUESTIONS

Will you kill me
 Before I die
Will you live with me
  As I live
You have feet
 Would you stand with me
You have hands
  Would you reach for me
You have voice
  Would you teach me
 These were questions
Found the answer
  But I still ask again ...

THE RISK

I know there's gotta be rain
If I love the rainbow
And I do
I know it's gotta be cold if I love the snow
And I do
I know it's gotta be hot if I love summer
I know the higher I climb the hill
The harder the wind blows
The faster I run
Even if am gonna fall
I still run to reach the light
There's always a risk
Don't ask me what
Just know
There's always The Risk

(try reading from the last line to the top)

TEARY HEART

Have you ever been broken
And then reply am fine
Have you ever smiled and laughed
Deep inside you just want to fall and cry
Have you ever been left in the dark, that the light
becomes so blinding , you don't want to go near it
Have you ever danced
Deep down you want to sleep and sulk

Just keep on dancing with that
Teary heart
Eyes filled with tears
Listen to the beat of your heart
And keep dancing
For one day
You will reply am fine sincerely
Your eyes will smile
Even with a tears of joy
Wailing from them
Your heart will smile
You will look at the mirror
And see the new smiling you
Who smiles in the mist of cries.

About the Author

Priscilla Akposi is a young lover of God who likes to explore writing. She lives in Calabar and is a student of the University of Calabar currently undergoing a five year program in Medical Laboratory Science. She hails from Akamkpa Local Government Area. She is a naturalist whose primary aim is to envelope minds with interesting life changing lessons and facts through her writing. She has many unpublished stories, poems, and songs which she is looking towards publishing.

www.ingramcontent.com/pod-product-compliance
Lightning Source LLC
LaVergne TN
LVHW010110170826
845678LV00012B/2339

* 9 7 8 1 9 6 0 0 3 8 4 8 7 *